TALL STACKS

A
Celebration
of
America's
Steamboat
Heritage

by J. Miles Wolf

Wolf Publishing Company

TALL
STACKS

A

Celebration

of

America's

Steamboat

Heritage

by J. Miles Wolf

Wolf Publishing Company

PHOTOGRAPHS by:

J. Miles Wolf

Robert A. Flischel

Jeff Friedman

Chris Cone

Gary Kessler

Gregory E. Rust

Bill Swartz

Art Dickinson

Dave Steinbrunner

Kim Simmons

John Michael Krekeler

Walt Roycraft

Ron Forth

Tom Schiff

Brad Smith

Gorden Morioka

Sam A. Marshall

TEXT by Applied History Associates, Cincinnati Ohio

Daniel Hurley, introduction and

Susan Redman-Rengstorf, narrative copy

DESIGN by Zender + Associates

Owen Brock, Rick Albertson, Nancy McIntosh, Michele Miller

and Micah Zender

First published 1995 by Wolf Publishing Company

The photographs in this book, except where noted in the photographers' credits, were taken by J. Miles Wolf. All rights to the photographs remain in the possession of the individual photographers.

Library of Congress Cataloging-in-Publication Data
Main entry under title: TALL STACKS

ISBN 0-9647433-1-0

Printed in Hong Kong through Palace Press

Wolf Publishing Company
708 Walnut Street
Cincinnati, OH 45202
(513) 381-3222
800-492-5105

SPECIAL THANKS to: Maura Wolf, Paula Wolf, Scott A. Wolf, Jeffrey S. Bakst, Ruth Perlman, Mike Zender, Jeff Fine, Richard Lewis, Rick Greiwe, Brian Becker, Kelly Kolar, Laura Davis, and all the staff and volunteers that make Tall Stacks possible.

REMEMBRANCES

by Daniel Hurley

As the bright October sun warmed away the last powdery wisps of the morning fog, the Schneider family eagerly stepped onto the pedestrian sidewalk of the Suspension Bridge. They decided the best way to start their visit to Tall Stacks was by parking in Covington and walking across John Roebling's Suspension Bridge, which had opened in 1867 at the peak of the Steamboat Age.

Stopping at midspan, the Schneiders took in the whole amazing scene. To their right, over in Newport, men dressed in Civil War uniforms were drilling and firing their muskets in front of a life-sized replica of the old Newport Barracks. The Barracks had dominated the Kentucky riverfront throughout the Nineteenth Century, but disappeared when the troops relocated to Ft. Thomas after the devastating floods of 1883 and 1884.

On the north shore, Cincinnati's Public Landing was already filled with thousands of people dressed in bright colored sweaters and windbreakers. "Look, Dad! There's the **Delta Queen**," cried Sarah. "You know Congress saved it. Oh, and look! Look over there, coming around the bend. That's the new **American Queen.** Wow! I thought the **Delta Queen** was big!"

"All I could see was people, I could feel the excitement in the pilot house."

Captain Gabrielle Chengery, *Delta Queen,* **1992**

PHOTOGRAPHS by:

J. Miles Wolf

Robert A. Flischel

Jeff Friedman

Chris Cone

Gary Kessler

Gregory E. Rust

Bill Swartz

Art Dickinson

Dave Steinbrunner

Kim Simmons

John Michael Krekeler

Walt Roycraft

Ron Forth

Tom Schiff

Brad Smith

Gorden Morioka

Sam A. Marshall

TEXT by Applied History Associates, Cincinnati Ohio

Daniel Hurley, introduction and

Susan Redman-Rengstorf, narrative copy

DESIGN by Zender + Associates

Owen Brock, Rick Albertson, Nancy McIntosh, Michele Miller

and Micah Zender

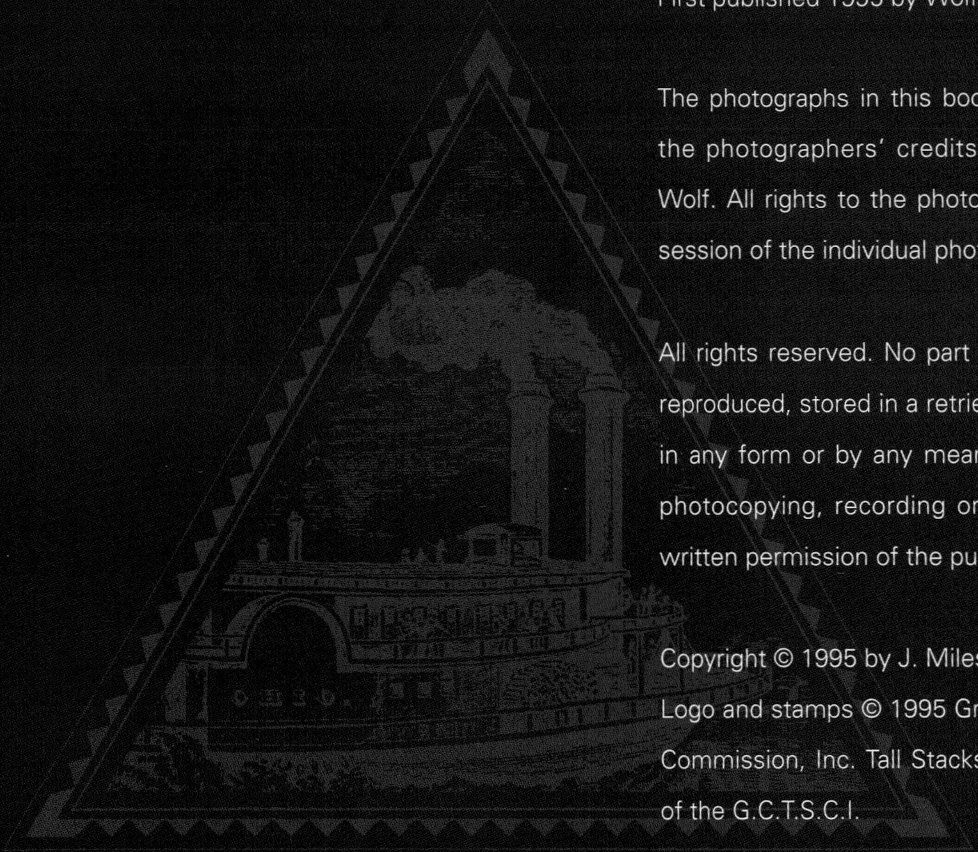

First published 1995 by Wolf Publishing Company

Wolf Publishing Company
708 Walnut Street
Cincinnati, OH 45202
(513) 381-3222
800-492-5105

Library of Congress Cataloging-in-Publication Data
Main entry under title: TALL STACKS

ISBN 0-9647433-1-0

Printed in Hong Kong through Palace Press

SPECIAL THANKS to: Maura Wolf, Paula Wolf, Scott A. Wolf, Jeffrey S. Bakst, Ruth Perlman, Mike Zender, Jeff Fine, Richard Lewis, Rick Greiwe, Brian Becker, Kelly Kolar, Laura Davis, and all the staff and volunteers that make Tall Stacks possible.

America's great inland rivers — the Ohio, Missouri and Mississippi — as well as hundreds of lesser watery ribbons of commerce were filled with an incredible array of "packet boats."

Modern excursion boats are designed to carry relaxed passengers in comfort, whether for a two hour dinner cruise or week-long vacation. Nineteenth century packets were work horses on which passengers had to share space and sacrifice comfort to accommodate valuable cargo. If Sarah's grandmother had traveled in 1855 from Cincinnati to New Orleans on the **Queen City**, she might not have found it so romantic. Taking a walk on the main deck required that she pick her way through bales of cotton, stacks of live chickens in coops, barrels of nails, and piles of lumber. And if her husband couldn't afford the more expensive tickets, he would have been required to go ashore with the crew

in the "wooding" party to replenish the fuel needed to satisfy the packet's ravenous engines.

The packets that worked America's inland rivers were an ingenious design. They resembled no other kind of boat. Unlike ocean-going vessels with their pointed hulls slicing 10 to 30 feet below the water line, the Western Packet was a flat bottomed contraption that might rise three, four or five stories above the water, but rode a mere 15 inches to five feet below the water. In fact, old time steamboaters liked to say that packets floated "on" the river not "in" it.

The genius behind the Western Packet was Captain Henry Shreve who developed this basic design around 1817 for very practical reasons. Just as today's excursion boats offer distorted echoes of nineteenth century packets, today's Ohio River gives a distorted image of the nineteenth century river.

In the mid-nineteenth century, in the Steamboat Era, the Ohio regularly dropped so low in the late Summer and Fall that the packets were forced into port for weeks at a time. In some stretches of the river, steamboats were at risk of running aground practically all

year around. The ideal packet was one that could travel on a heavy dew!

The modern high lift concrete dams built since 1950 have transformed the Ohio into a string of relatively stable lakes. The river occasionally floods, but it no longer drops to an unnavigable level, even during severe droughts like that in 1988.

A well-built packet was a technological wonder and an aesthetic marvel. Each boat required the combined skills of nearly 500 craftsmen using hand tools but no

blueprints. The moment of truth was the launch. According to steamboat historian Jack Custer, "Being able to jack up 500 tons of wood five feet in the air and have it slide down a ramp is almost inconceivable now. For about 10 seconds, it belongs in the hands of God, no man could control it."

Between 1817 and 1885 the art of building packets for America's inland rivers flourished in dozens of places along the Ohio, Mississippi and Missouri Rivers. At mid-century in Cincinnati, boat yards, saw mills and foundries stretched from the eastern edge of the

Public Landing for several miles through the East End.

But the old packets were only part of the story of the Steamboat Age. Equally fascinating were the men and women who lived on and around these boats. Perched in the pilothouse high above the river, the captains and pilots were lords of a very special realm. They were always scanning ahead, reading the river. Pilots tried to anticipate a host of problems. Unmapped sandbars dissolved and reformed constantly. Trees washed off the shore, jammed into the sandy bottom and lurked just below the surface waiting to rip gaping holes in passing hulls. Banks of fog could make it impossible to see past the roof of the Hurricane deck, while ice could freeze the boat in place for weeks and then crush its hull into match sticks when it broke up. Despite these challenges, Captain Fred Way summed up the life of a steamboat captain as "being bored to death 90 percent of the time and scared to death 10 percent of the time."

Below the pilothouse the crew on a packet made up a floating community. The face and chest of the firemen could blister before the blazing furnace while their backs were pelted with sleet and rain. Although the

time chewing tobacco and debating the wisdom of the Kansas-Nebraska Act. But others, dressed in dirty cotton pants and speaking English with heavy Gaelic accents, or German, or Yiddish stayed out on deck day and night seated among all their worldly possessions watching wide-eyed as the vast promising expanses of the New World slid silently past.

Tall Stacks, the modern celebration of the Steamboat Age in America, began as one of four major events sponsored by the Greater Cincinnati Bicentennial Commission in 1988. Fourteen boats and nearly a million people participated. The enthusiastic response of people to the color, excitement and pageantry of Tall Stacks inspired its organizers to immediately start planning for their return.

Four years later, Tall Stacks II drew 17 boats and 1.2 million people to the banks of the Ohio. Covington and Newport built their celebration of Kentucky's Bicentennial around Tall Stacks. A street fair stretched the length of Riverside Drive in Covington, while Newport sponsored a Civil War encampment in Taylor Park.

river was primarily a man's world, women were often hired as cooks. And as Captain Dana Young saw it, "The cook is the most important person on the boat. If you don't have a good cook, you have crew trouble right away."

The roustabouts, African-American men known only by nicknames like Red Shirt, Tar Eye, Stoogie and Rock, slept on the deck in good weather and near the engines when it turned cold. They loaded and unloaded tons of cargo on their shoulders and backs, while working to the rhythm of songs that spoke of home and family.

Even the passengers were a colorful lot. Some of the women in wide hoop skirts spent their days knitting and reading in the Ladies Parlor, while some of the men dressed in silk vests and fine coats spent their

On the Ohio shore, Tom Sawyerville opened in Bicentennial Commons. This whimsical activity area allowed younger children to get involved on their own level with the sights, sounds and images of the Steamboat Age.

Tall Stacks III will be celebrated in mid October, 1995. This time 21 boats are scheduled, and 1.8 million people are expected to cruise, dine and tour the magnificent sternwheelers. Over the seven years since the first Tall Stacks, the event's reputation has grown and spread. Many of the visitors expected in 1995 will travel not only from the East and West coasts of the United States, but from Europe and Asia as well.

At the end of the Twentieth Century, when astronauts routinely orbit the Earth at speeds of 17,500 mph, and race car drivers whip around the Indianapolis Speedway at more than 220 mph, why do almost two million people flock to the Cincinnati riverfront during Tall Stacks to watch steamboats race each other at seven mph?

For some, it's a nostalgic plunge into a romanticized past that seems to be devoid of the complexities of modern life. For others, it's a living history lesson, an opportunity to talk to captains who now steer with the help of radar, but can talk knowledgeably about the challenges their predecessors faced 150 years ago.

But for the really lucky ones, like the Schneiders, Tall Stacks is first and foremost an opportunity to get family members to really talk across the vast gaps that rarely get bridged in ordinary life. When they crossed the Suspension Bridge in the morning, Sarah did most of the talking, mainly about facts she had learned in school. By the time they walked back over the bridge towards Kentucky that night, each one had gained new insights into each other and felt connected in new ways.

Diane, Sarah's mother, had never before heard her mother talk about how Diane's father had once dreamed of a musical career, or that he had been a good enough trumpet player in his college days to fill in a couple of times with a band on the **Island Queen**. Her husband, John, and son Michael were busy sketching designs inspired by the gingerbread woodwork of the steamboats. The long promised bookcases they planned to make together in the workshop were

going to end up a bit fancier than first imagined.

By the time they reached the car, Sarah's grandmother was physically exhausted, but profoundly happy. For years she hadn't even thought about, much less talked about, some of the stories of her life that she told that day. Only a few touched directly on boats or the river. But somehow Tall Stacks had sparked the interaction and built a bridge across the generations of the Schneider family even more beautiful and more enduring than the one built by John Roebling nearly 130 years ago.

S-T-E-A-M-BOAT A'COMIN'!!

"It's like planning a wedding. We're waiting for the guests. We've got everything ready, and we want to show off Cincinnati – Greater Cincinnati – to the rest of the world."

Barbara Jane England, Greater Cincinnati Convention and Visitors Bureau, 1992

The day is heavy with anticipation when the first sound of the calliope signals the opening of a Tall Stacks celebration in Cincinnati, Ohio. Steamboats big and small slide gracefully under the John A. Roebling Suspension Bridge. With paddle wheels churning, whistles screeching, and smokestacks belching, the "Parade of Tall Stacks" magically transforms the Port of Cincinnati back into the hustle and bustle of a by-gone era.

Welcome banners drop from the bridge while hundreds of thousands of riverboat enthusiasts of all ages pay tribute to America's rich river heritage. Once sturdy rulers of the inland waterways, steamboats today offer a nostalgic glimpse at the age of stern-wheelers.

"A steamboat, coming from New Orleans, brings to the remotest villages... and the very doors of cabins, a little Paris, a section of Broadway, or a slice of Philadelphia."

Western Monthly Review, 1827

Eager groups of "passbook" holders gather at the river's edge as early as 6:00 in the morning. For the next four hours, these lucky participants get to tour all but two Tall Stacks steamboats docked at the Public Landing. The **Mississippi Queen** and the **Delta Queen** are not open because of overnight passengers. As popular as these tours are, so too are the individual passbook "stamps" each person receives upon boarding a boat. For many, these stamps become lasting reminders of this special celebration. Three other types of boat tours — lunch, dinner, and moonlight tours — keep the event flowing smoothly.

"... *running all night, we found ourselves this morning within 12 or 15 miles of New Orleans but being surrounded with fog, the pilot after running the boat on shore two or three times came to the conclusion that he could not see to run the boat with steam so we floated for something like an hour — when the fog cleared away... to let us go ahead.*"

Joseph W. Fawcett, Journal 1840

"Our brass band plays at the principal points during the day and in the evening our excellent string band amuses the passengers in the cabin."

Capt. W. B. Miller, *Thompson Dean,* **1875**

Much of America's musical heritage was inspired as steamboats knitted together America's people. Indiana farmers plucked banjos on the long journey home from New Orleans. Immigrants sang songs from their homeland on the decks of boats heading west.

Rhythmic verses flowed from African-American roustabouts as they worked under the hot sun loading and unloading cargo. In later years, soft strains of the boat's orchestra entertained passengers in the first-class cabin. The same is true at Tall Stacks, where participants can choose from a kaleidoscope of entertainment, including traditional brass bands, Mississippi Delta Blues, and everything in between.

Perhaps the most enduring symbol of the steamboat era is the shrill melodies of the steam calliope. Famous for its off-key screeching and an ability to announce a boat's arrival from miles away, the calliope runs off the steam from the same boilers that turn the paddle wheel. When the calliope player presses down on a key, a burst of steam is pushed out of a brass or copper whistle making a loud, hollow sound. Of the boats at Tall Stacks, only a few, the **Belle of Louisville**, the **Delta Queen**, **Mississippi Queen**, and **The President**, have authentic steam calliopes.

"I call it a cross between an organ and a fire siren."

Travis C. Basconcelos, calliope player,
***Belle of Louisville*, 1992**

HISTORY COMES ALIVE

TRADITIONS

Hoop skirts and crinolines, top hats and cutaway coats, and even Civil War uniforms — all are a part of the human drama surrounding Tall Stacks. Hundreds of volunteers and visitors, some who hand stitched their own costumes, join in the spirit of reliving the past by "dressing up" and strolling along the riverbanks on both sides of the Ohio River. Colorful period clothes and a wide array of accessories lend an air of authenticity to the Tall Stacks celebration.

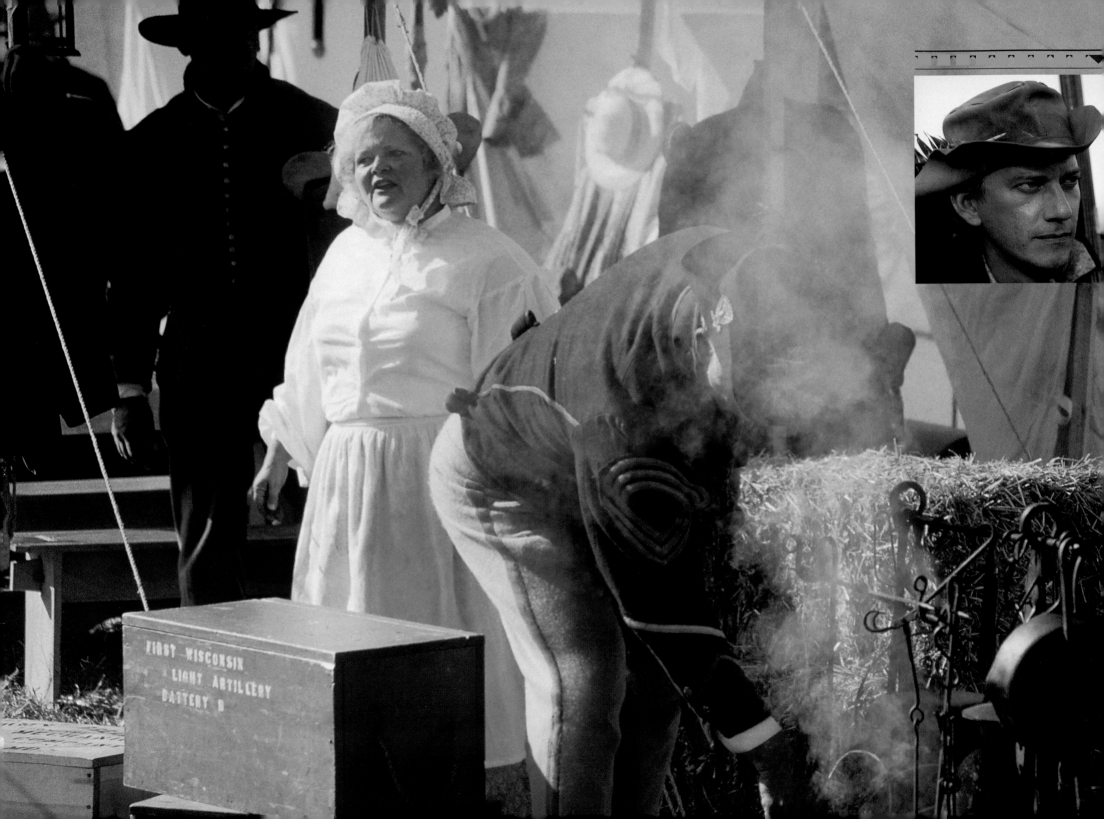

In 1988, Tall Stacks coincided with Cincinnati's Bicentennial celebration. In 1992, Tall Stacks tied into Kentucky's year-long Bicentennial. Local organizers created an array of living history activities along the Kentucky shore of the Ohio River. The most dramatic was the depiction of everyday military life at the recreated Newport Barracks, a major 19th century military outpost. Civil War reenactment groups from all over Ohio, Kentucky and Indiana converged at the point where the Ohio and Licking Rivers meet, and for four days, lived in tents, cooked over open fires, drilled with muskets and fired cannons.

"We got into Cincinnati two days ago and ever since I've felt like I'm back 100 years ago. This is what it must have been like."

Captain Gabrielle Chengery, *Delta Queen,* **1992**

"*Where else would you see newsboys in knickers hawking newpapers proclaiming baseball's first international World Series? Or Mark Twain look-a-likes using camcorders? Or women wearing Scarlett O'Hara dresses with 35-mm cameras swinging from their necks?*"

Cincinnati Enquirer, October 1992

Tall Stacks visitors are "going to see a military camp with tents set up. They'll see activities that the soldiers would have done. They'll see officers' wives dressed up in their fancy hoop skirts."

**Captain Allen Dorsett,
Union Army's 18th Indiana Light Artillery**

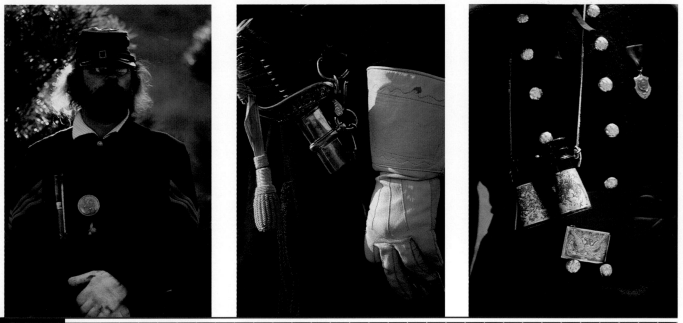

GATHERIN' AT THE RIVER

The shores of Cincinnati and Northern Kentucky are awash in a sea of color. Hundreds of thousands of steamboat enthusiasts move in for a firsthand glimpse of both the grandiose and work-a-day riverboats of Tall Stacks. A sea of people ebb and flow among the recreated turquoise blue smokestacks dotting the Public Landing and wait patiently to board a boat, buy a souvenir, or simply find a seat to relax with a cool drink. The boats, decked out in bright red, white and blue bunting, also contribute to the festive atmosphere.

Throughout the celebration, boats are packed with eager passengers arriving and departing at the Public Landing. Popular short river tours as well as half-day cruises have been sold out for months. Good food and entertainment, and the chance to meet new friends, are all perks of those lucky enough to travel on one of the luxurious "Queens" of the river. Everyone has a chance to imagine the romance of 19th century riverboat travel — if only for a short time.

"At each (meal) there are a great many small dishes and plates upon the table, and very little in them; so that although there is every appearance of a mighty 'spread,' there is seldom really more than a joint."

Charles Dickens, *American Notes for General Circulation*, 1848

"That's what I like, the pipes; it sounds like an organ... The color, the flags and the music make it special. It's different from anything else."

Keith Lanning, Brookville, Indiana

Tall Stacks is not all glamour and romance. Behind the scenes, celebration organizers handle thousands of challenges quietly and efficiently. The impact of a million visitors over a short period is dramatic — traffic jams on the roadways and the waterways, booked-up hotels for miles around, parking problems, and last but not least, a mountain of garbage! Everyday on the boats alone, crews prepare and serve over 4,000 meals and countless servings of snacks, coffee, tea, beer and soft drinks. On both sides of the Ohio River, food and drink booths keep hopping as hungry festival-goers stop to refuel. Garbage collection is on a strict schedule to keep the grounds and the visiting fleet of boats clean.

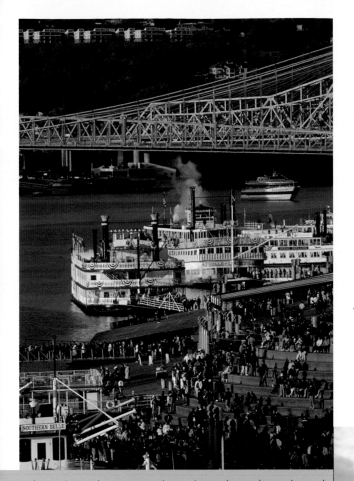

"I guess you miss the fun and flavor of the event, but meeting all the new people and being around the action is probably just as much fun as the event itself."

Al Judy, Tall Stacks volunteer, 1988

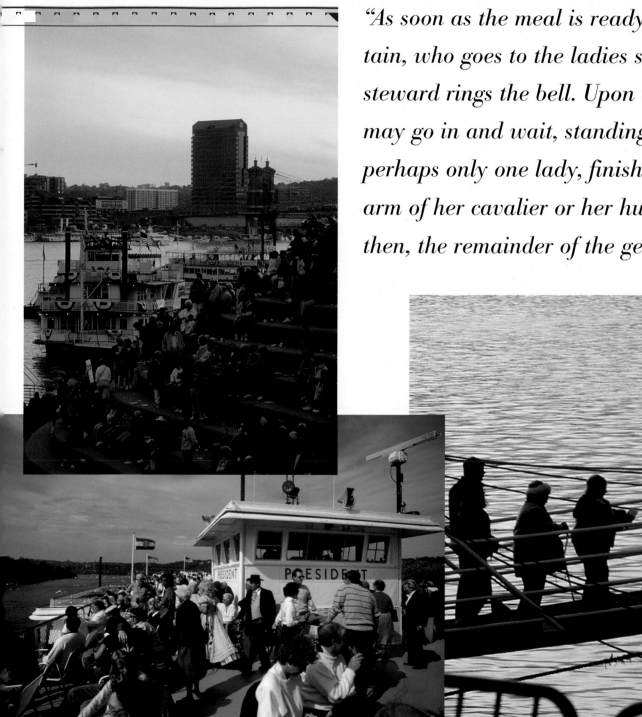

"*As soon as the meal is ready to be served, the steward informs the captain, who goes to the ladies saloon and invites them to the table. The steward rings the bell. Upon that announcement, the unmarried men may go in and wait, standing as patient as sheep, until the ladies, or perhaps only one lady, finishes her toilette, sweeps to the table on the arm of her cavalier or her husband, and sits down; then, and not until then, the remainder of the gentlemen take their seats.*"

Journal of Randolph Frederick Kurz, 1846-52

PLAYIN' BY THE RIVER

Throughout the 19th century, youngsters dreamed of piloting long, towering river Queens up and down the zig-zaggy routes of America's inland rivers, steering clear of snags and tree trunks, working hard to avoid sandbars, learning to "read" the river during the night as well as the day, and finally, arriving at port with all the fanfare usually reserved for visiting dignitaries. Mark Twain was one such boy who dreamed, and worked, on riverboats. The adventures of some of Twain's most famous characters, like Tom Sawyer and Becky Thatcher, come to life in "Tom Sawyerville," a river town first introduced at Tall Stacks 1992. Here, young visitors can explore the scary "McDougal's Cave" with its bats and warning signs to "Look Out for Injun Joe."

"I liked what the signs said. It wasn't really scary. We've got the book (Tom Sawyer) in our room. Yeah, maybe I'll read it now."

Mike Wallace, age 9,

Union Elementary School, Union, Kentucky

Tall Stacks offers something for everyone. Sack races, musical entertainment, and demonstrations help youngsters relive the days of long ago. Moms and dads participate with their children as grandparents and other family members cheer from the sidelines. School groups from Ohio, Kentucky and Indiana come to Tall Stacks to participate in special group activities and discover firsthand how steamboats forged a new American nation. A perfect complement to any school's curriculum, Tall Stacks presents an exciting opportunity for teachers to involve their students through a unique day-long experience.

"When I was a boy, there was but one permanent ambition among my comrades in our village on the west bank of the Mississippi River. That was, to be a steamboatman."

Mark Twain, *Life on the Mississippi,* **1883**

WORKIN' ON THE RIVER

Steamboat lore is full of romance and elegance, yet working on the river was another matter. Until the late 19th century, packets made their real money from delivering goods and products to various markets — not from carrying passengers. Often, steamboats were loaded bottom to top with crates and barrels leaving little room for movement. Crews worked around the clock piloting the boat, stoking the fires in the boilers, feeding and entertaining passengers, and loading and unloading cargo. It was a hard, mostly routine, but sometimes very exciting, life. Other than transporting cargo, not much has changed about working on a steamboat — it's still an around-the-clock job.

Delta Queen "crew member Doug Kellum of New Orleans, who is on 'fire watch,' steps down narrow, hot steel steps into the guts of the boat. As he descends, the room gets darker and hotter. The monstrous roar of the boiler never stops."

Cincinnati Enquirer, October, 1992

Just as the boats depend on their crews to run successfully, the Tall Stacks Commission depends on its staff and volunteers. Starting in 1988 with the first Tall Stacks celebration, 4,000 volunteers were on hand to serve 56,000 ticket holders, 25,000 Passport Tourists, and 919,000 visitors. Four years later, in 1992, a volunteer planning committee of 500 put in more than 10,000 hours in the preparation, and training of some 7,000 volunteers. Services range from stamping passports, directing pedestrian traffic and leading activities to simply answering questions for the more than one million participants.

"I wish they'd do Tall Stacks every year!"

Charles Ballinger, Avondale, 1992

BELLES AND QUEENS

"*This town loves the river. That's why this works.*

Everyone from taxicab drivers to kids, to the people running it are into it."

Captain Ken Goldfine, *Southern Belle*

Tall Stacks has a lot to offer — good food, entertainment, tours and demonstrations — but the main draw of the event is the boats, big and small. Representing one of the most productive periods of American history, steamboats stand as a testament to early American technology and achievement. Gracefully towering over America's waterways, steamboats single-handily, and practically overnight, turned lazy one-way rivers into fast, two-way highways propelling the United States through the 19th century. Tall stacks offers a rare chance to meet and greet up close these "Queens & Belles" of the rivers, and to pay tribute to their contributions.

One of the youngest, and yet most famous, of the Tall Stacks boats is the **Mississippi Queen**. Modeled after traditional Mississippi riverboats, the **Mississippi Queen** was designed by London naval architect John Gardner specifically for tourist travel on America's rivers. Built in Jeffersonville, Indiana, in 1973-75, the boat is 382 feet long and has seven enclosed decks with room for over 400 overnight passengers. With its steam condensing engines and two water tube boilers, the double-stepped paddle wheels run on a common shaft. Christened at Louisville, Kentucky, in July 1976 the **Mississippi Queen** has always called New Orleans, Louisiana, its home port.

At 285 feet long, the **Delta Queen** has four enclosed decks and carries 180 overnight passengers. Assembled in 1926 in California with parts fabricated in Glasgow, Scotland, the **Delta Queen**, and its twin the **Delta King**, each cost $875,000 — the most expensive and luxurious steamboats on America's rivers. In 1946, the **Delta Queen** was sold to Greene Line Steamers, Inc. in Cincinnati, Ohio where it started offering tourist excursions of the Ohio, Mississippi, Tennessee and Cumberland rivers. Today a national historic landmark, a 1971 presidential sanction enabled the **Delta Queen** to continue as the last wooden-hulled steamboat carrying overnight passengers. The boat, now owned by the Delta Queen Company and docked in New Orleans, Louisiana, still proudly bears the inscription, "Port of Cincinnati."

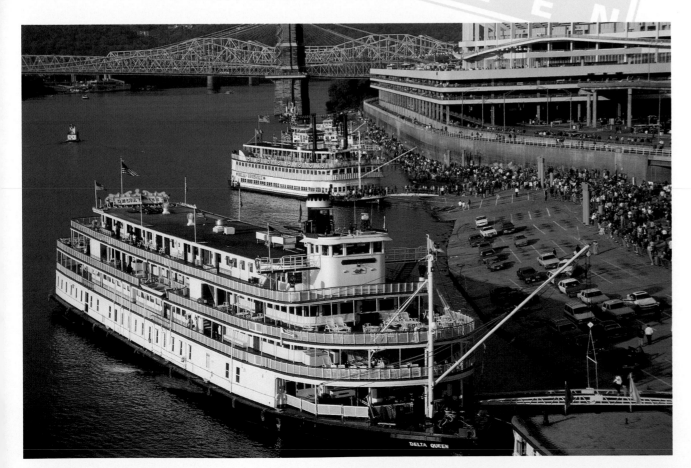

"Out here watching the Earth go by on a steamboat, you don't really want to go back." **Passenger, *Delta Queen***

"*If they want us back, we'll be back.*" **Captain Mike Fitzgerald,** *Belle of Louisville,* **1992**

The **Belle of Louisville**, stretching 191.5 feet and carrying 800 passengers for short-term excursions, is one of the oldest boats at Tall Stacks. Built at Pittsburgh in 1914 for the Memphis Packet Company, she was first called the **Idlewild** and worked as a packet, excursion boat and ferry. Rechristened the **Avalon** in 1948 and later based in Cincinnati, the boat offered excursions on the Mississippi, Ohio and Kanawha Rivers. In 1962, the boat was purchased by the Jefferson County, Kentucky, Fiscal Court and was renamed for a third time — the **Belle of Louisville**. An extensive renovation in 1968 updated the **Belle** by lengthening her bow and installing three new Western-style boilers. Despite all these changes, her paddle wheels are still driven by the Rees high-pressure engines originally installed in 1915.

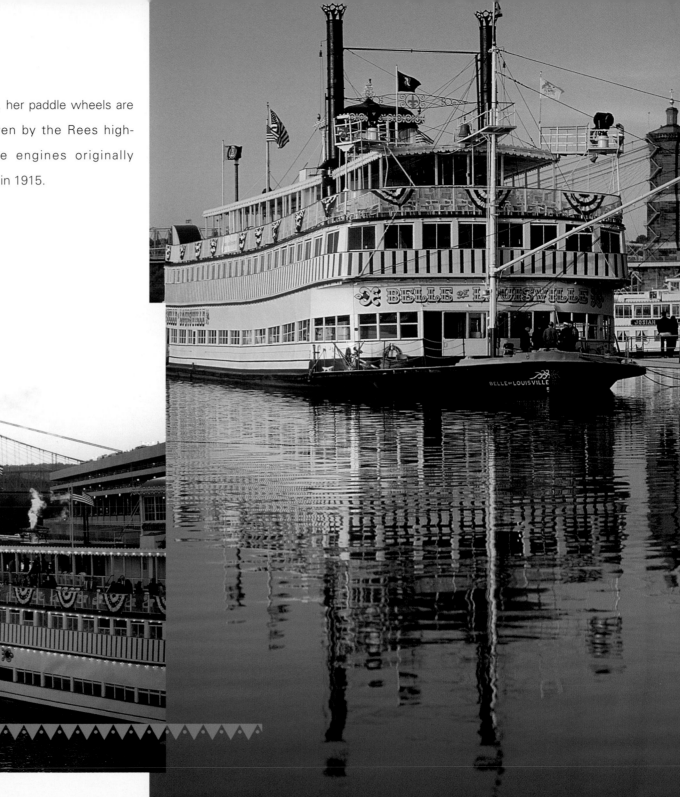

*"With its double landing stages, wedding-cake composition, tall smokestacks and decorated pilot house, the **American Queen** will rival the famous **J. M. White** as the ultimate expression of steam-boatin' luxury and grace."*

Al Luthmers, The Delta Queen Steamboat Company

Traveling from ports across the country — from St. Paul, Minnesota, to New Orleans, Louisiana — and all points in between, riverboats big and small depart their home ports in a race to Cincinnati, Beckoned by the Tall Stacks celebration, captains of boats of all sizes and horsepower test their piloting skills and plot a course down- or upriver through locks and dams. From the grand 382 foot deck of the **Mississippi Queen** to the charming 77 foot deck of the **Spirit of Cincinnati**, these boats represent the finest paddle wheelers working America's rivers today. Throughout their stay, each is a welcomed and honored guest at the Port of Cincinnati and Tall Stacks.

"*Yeah. it's been harried as hell and we've loved it.*"

Captain William D. Bowell, *Johnathan Paddleford*

On your mark, get set, go! Long a riverboat tradition, riverboat racing is at its best at Tall Stacks. Boats race in three heats upriver from the Public Landing, turning at Schmidt Field, and then racing to cross the finish line under the L & N Bridge. Passengers and festival goers join in the thrill as they watch first-time match-ups between the **Southern Belle,** the **Mark Twain,** and the **Becky Thatcher**. In the final race, the traditional rivalry of the **Delta Queen** and **Belle of Louisville** is dramatically played out in a contest for riverboat racing's highest reward — the coveted Golden Antlers — a symbol of the deer's graceful speed.

"I thought it was very exciting. I started from the end of the Landing and ran all the way up to the finish line yelling and screaming. Yelling, 'Come on, Come on!'"

Steamboat racing fan, 1988

"… *The steamboats were finer than anything on shore. Compared with superior dwelling houses and first-class hotels in the valley, they were indubitably magnificent, they were 'palaces'…*"

Mark Twain

EVENING FALLS

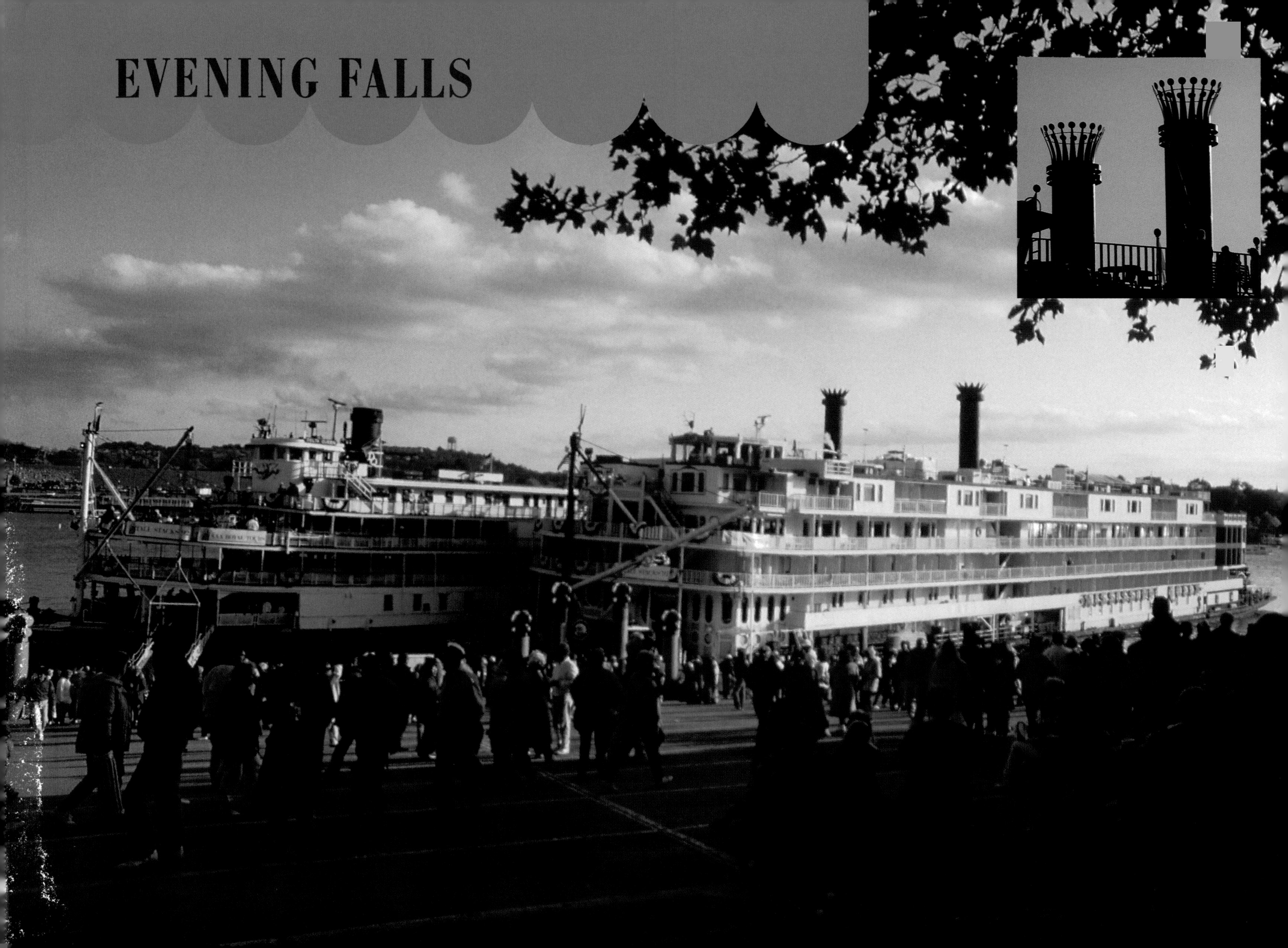

> *"Supper is now announced, and we go in to do it justice. The long cabin is filled from end to end with tables. The linen is spotless, the silver, china and glass shine in attractive beauty, and the white-jacketed waiters stand ready to serve us. The bill-of-fare is varied, abundant and excellent."*
>
> **Pittsburgh and Cincinnati Packet Company,** *Souvenir Program,* **1895**

The shadows cast by a setting sun greet late afternoon cruises as Tall Stacks riverboats return to port. Throughout the history of steamboating, late afternoon often marked the end of a long work day on the river with boats pulling into port to unload cargo and passengers. But at Tall Stacks, the end of the day signals a burst of new activity for the million Tall Stacks visitors as yesterday's riverboats mix pleasantly with the sleek pleasure craft of today — all swaying gently in perfect time with the natural rhythms of the Ohio River.

"It had to be one of the hottest tickets in town this weekend… the Captain's table on the President."

Michael Collins, reporter, WLWT-TV, 1988

As dusk descends, boats push off from the Public Landing beginning Moonlight Tours offering breathtaking views of the Cincinnati skyline aglow with millions of lights and the evening charm of Covington's historic Riverside Drive. Dinner and dancing revive the days when excursion boats provided pleasant diversions from the hustle and bustle of everyday life.

"Once or twice of a night we would see a steamboat slipping along in the dark...and then she would belch a whole world of sparks up out of her chimbleys, and they would rain down in the river and look awful pretty..."

Huck Finn, *The Adventures of Huck Finn,* **1883**

The true romance of the steamboat era plays out dramatically after the sun sets over the Queen City and Northern Kentucky. Hundreds of lights from boats and buildings twinkle brightly against the recreated facades of Cincinnati's Public Landing in 1850 and the riverfronts of Newport and Covington. The evening falls covering the river with a blanket of darkness — quietly ending yet another nostalgic trip back in time.

It's still dark, and everything is quiet, when the alarm goes off at 5:00 a.m. A quick shower, a glass of juice — just enough time to grab the equipment and load the van. Driving down to the riverside in Newport, Kentucky, its dark and cold on this crisp, clear October morning.

On the river's edge, the water is rushing along, and in the distance I can hear the steady movement and quiet hum of trucks and buses buzzing across the bridges. The sky is slowly brightening as the sun works its way up on the horizon. After setting up the tripod and carefully placing the large format 4x5 camera on top, I level and adjust the camera and I am ready to go to work.

In an instant, the scene rapidly unfolds before me. The lights of the steamboats and riverboats of Tall Stacks twinkle and glow casting a beautiful reflection on the Ohio River. The calliope's music signals the start of a new day. As the light level increases, I can just start to make out the shapes of people walking on the decks of boats and all over the Public Landing and Serpentine Wall. I check the final focus on the ground-glass of my camera. The sky is now a brilliant sapphire blue as I expose my first sheet of film. The sun finally hits the horizon filling the scene with golden light. Cincinnati's skyline and the boats glow with amazing light. I quickly expose several more sheets of film (see pages 82-83), hesitating for just a moment to soak up the beauty and uniqueness of the event.

Quickly, I pack up my equipment and drive across the L&N Bridge to the Ohio side of the river. I park my van off to the side of the road and from an elevated viewpoint look down on the sights and sounds below me — it's unbelievable. The riverfront is already filled with thousands of people on the Serpentine Wall, many of them getting their passports stamped and boarding the boats for a firsthand look. I set up my tripod and 35mm camera and start composing and shooting all the color and action I see (page 70). In just 10 minutes, I've used four different lenses and two rolls of film documenting this setting of endless photographic possibilites. The excitement and energy I experienced at this spot is a feeling I will never forget. Then it's off to the crowds to explore and document this historic event.

J. Miles Wolf

The following donated their time and talents to photographing the Tall Stacks Festivals. Their visions, their angles, and the light and emotion they captured create the visual memories that will now stay with all of us through the publication of this book.

All the photographs in this book are copyrighted by the individual photographers. All rights are reserved by these individual photographers. No photographs may be reproduced in any manner without written permission of the photographers.

All photographs not listed below are ©1995 J. Miles Wolf.

Plus an additional 75 photographs not listed on the photographers credits pages.

◄ A 1988 multiple exposure by J. Miles Wolf which was sealed in the City Hall Time Capsule that will be opened in the year 2088.

TOM SCHIFF ©1995

SAM A. MARSHALL ©1995

Sam Marshall, Cincinnati

BRAD SMITH ©1995

PhotoSmith Photography, Cincinnati

Delta Queen Steamboat Co., New Orleans, LA.

* Full page photographs

Contemporary quotes are drawn from the Cincinnati Enquirer, the Cincinnati Post, the Kentucky Post, WLW-TV and WKRC-TV.

GORDON MORIOKA ©1995

Gorden Morioka Photography, Cincinnati

This book captures the spirit of the Tall Stacks celebration, a signature event for our great city. The award-winning selection of photographs showcases the beautiful setting of our community and the drama of its steamboating era.

Thank you to the photographers who provided their talent and images to this book. They are the artists that enable us to enjoy the memories of Tall Stacks and allow us to proclaim that Cincinnati is America's most picturesque inland river city.

Richard J. Greiwe
Executive Director
Greater Cincinnati Tall Stacks Commission